A New True Book

THE SEMINOLE

By Emilie U. Lepthien

 CHILDRENS PRESS™

CHICAGO

Seminole Indian woman at work

*To Alice M. Bauer in appreciation
for miles traveled together*

Library of Congress Cataloging in Publication Data

Lepthien, Emilie U. (Emilie Utteg)
    The Seminole.

    (A New true book)
    Includes index.

    Summary: Presents a history of the Seminole Indians.
    1. Seminole Indians—History—Juvenile literature.
[1. Seminole Indians—History. 2. Indians of North
America—History] I. Title.
E99.S28L47 1985   975.9'00497   84-23141
ISBN 0-516-01941-4   AACR2

TABLE OF CONTENTS

The Timucaua Indians lived in Tampa Bay, in central Florida. Hernando de Soto met them when he explored Florida in 1539. A display (above) at the south Florida Museum shows a Timucaua brave dressed for a wedding ceremony. Some Seminole live in the Everglades (below).

THE FIRST SEMINOLE

The Seminole Indians did not always live in Florida. They once were part of the Creek tribe that lived and farmed in southern Georgia and Alabama.

When the European settlers came to America, they took over the Indians' farmland. They made some

Flag of the Seminole

of the Indians slaves. They forced others to move farther south.

When they lost their farms, some of the Creek moved into Florida.

The Creek who stayed behind called these Indians Sem-in-ole, meaning wanderer or runaway.

EARLY SEMINOLE LIFE

In Florida, some Creek Indians married Indians from other tribes. They built log cabins and started to farm. They began a new life and a new tribe, the Seminole.

Seminole log cabin

1910 photograph of Willie Cypress poling his canoe in the Florida Everglades.

Each family had its own small vegetable garden. But the tribe also had a community farm.

The men fished in a nearby lake and hunted in the forest. There was grazing land for cattle and horses.

BLACKS AND THE SEMINOLE

Some black slaves escaped from Georgia and Alabama plantations. They fled to Florida. The Seminole welcomed the runaways.

The blacks worked for the Seminole. Some were slaves, but were treated more like tenant farmers.

Cootie Johnson, a Creek freeman, was the official lawyer of the Western Seminole tribe during the oil boom days in the Indian territory.

After a time, some of the blacks owned their own farms, had their own villages, and elected their own chiefs. Some married Seminole.

The plantation owners wanted their slaves back. They asked the United States government to send troops to Florida to get them.

Florida still belonged to Spain. But in 1812 and 1813 U. S. troops did go into Florida. They caught very few slaves.

Wearing traditional Seminole clothes,
Willie Cypress (left) skins a wild turkey.
Seminole women (above) grind corn
by hand.

THE FIRST
SEMINOLE WAR

More white settlers came
to Florida and saw the
good Seminole farms. They
wanted that land, too.

The Seminole refused to give up their land. They fought the settlers.

In 1817, General Andrew Jackson led three thousand soldiers into Florida. The troops burned Seminole villages. They took thousands of bushels of corn. They took the Seminole cattle, hogs, and horses.

The Seminole were forced to move farther

south again. In 1819 the
United States bought
Florida from Spain. By
1822, Florida became a
territory of the United
States. Thousands of new
settlers moved into Florida.
They wanted the Seminole
land.

Some Seminole signed a
treaty with the United
States. They agreed to give
up thirty-two million acres
of land. In exchange the

Seminole Indian family

Indians would receive four
million acres farther south.
Most of the Seminole
were very angry. They said
the Seminole men did not
have the right to sign the

Red mangrove and sawgrass (above) in Everglades National Park. Andrew Jackson (right) was president of the United States from 1829 to 1837.

treaty. The land they were to receive was swampy, and could not be farmed.

But the Indians were forced to move again. Without good farmland, they were soon hungry. They became desperate. But there was no place they could turn for help.

THE SECOND SEMINOLE WAR

Andrew Jackson, now president of the United States, ordered all of the southeastern Indians to move west of the Mississippi River.

The Seminole and other Indians (the Cherokee, Creek, Choctaw, and Chickamauga) were told to move.

Some Seminole agreed to move. But not Osceola.

A portrait of Osceola was painted by George Catlin.

Osceola felt the land in Florida rightfully belonged to his people. He refused to move. In 1835, the second Seminole War began.

The war was fought from 1835 to 1842. There were

The Seminole would attack and then disappear into the Big Cypress Swamp.

many battles between the Seminole and the U. S. troops. Often the Indians were successful. They knew the land well. They could strike and disappear into the swamp.

Finally Chief Micanopy said the Seminole wanted

Seminole Indian
dressed for battle

peace. Even Osceola
agreed to move west.

Then Osceola learned
that his black friends could
not go west with the
Seminole. The blacks
would be returned to
slavery.

Osceola and his braves decided to stay with their friends. The Seminole War continued.

In October, 1837, Osceola agreed to meet and talk to an American general. He and his braves were told they would be safe if they carried a white flag of truce. But the Indians were tricked. They were captured.

Osceola became ill and died in 1838. Osceola was buried at Fort Moultrie. His

Seminole family walks through the swamp.

headstone reads "Patriot and Warrior."

The Seminole continued to fight. It was a losing battle. By 1842, most of the Seminole were dead or had been moved to what was called Indian Territory.

Wearing a soldier's uniform from the 1830s,
a guide tells a visitor about life at Fort Foster.

The trip west was long and hard. Many died on the way.

Not all the Seminole left Florida. A small band fled into Big Cypress and the Everglades swamps. Descendants of those Indians still live in Florida.

LIFE IN THE SWAMPS

The Seminole built villages on ground dry enough for farming. They planted corn and vegetables. They also raised some fruit.

They lived in huts called chickees. These huts had raised platforms with open sides and roofs thatched with palmetto leaves.

The chickees were comfortable at night. The

Seminole chickee

wind could blow through.
The Indians slept in
hammocks. There was
almost no other furniture in
the chickees. Most of the
day was spent working
outdoors.

THE THIRD SEMINOLE WAR

In 1855 some surveyors made camp near a Seminole village. They stole the Indians' crops.

Chief Billy Bowlegs asked the men to pay for what they had taken. The surveyors refused.

As a result, the third Seminole War began. It lasted three years.

An old sketch
of Billy Bowlegs

In 1858 the Western Seminole convinced Chief Billy Bowlegs and about 150 Seminole to move west to Indian Territory. But about three hundred would not leave.

THE SEMINOLE
IN THE WEST

The Western Seminole called themselves the Seminole Nation.

In 1905, the Five Civilized Tribes—the Cherokee, Creek, Choctaw, Chickamauga, and Seminole—asked Congress to form an all-Indian state. They wanted the state to be named "Sequoyah," after a famous Cherokee. In 1906 Congress

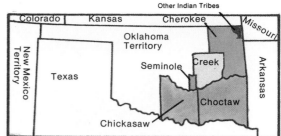

In Wewoka, Oklahoma in 1902 the tribe voted for the chief of the Seminole Nation. Men for each candidate lined up on opposite sides of the street. Then the count was made to decide the winner (left).
The Five Civilized Tribes occupied most of the Indian Territory in 1906. Only the northeast corner was for other Indian Tribes (above).

refused to grant them statehood. Non-Indians wanted to move into the territory because oil and gas had been discovered.

Oklahoma became a state in 1907. It was formed from Indian and Oklahoma territories.

At the Tampa reservation a Seminole (left)
shows how alligators (right) are captured.

FLORIDA SEMINOLES

The Seminole who
moved into the Florida
swamplands had to change
their way of life. They
learned to catch alligators.
Fishing and hunting were

INDIAN WORDS

Children	Who-Pish-Co-Cha
Little Boy	Nag-Noo-Che
Little Girl	Ta-Goo-Che
My Wife	Cha-Hai-Kee
My Husband	Nu Nack-Nee
Sister	Cha-Foon-Kee
Brother	Cha-Ta-Che-Kee
Man	Nack-Kee
Woman	Ta-Kee
Mother	Wa-A-Chee
Father	Ta-Tee
Red People	Ya-Ate-Key-Tische
White	Ya-Ate-Not-Key
Colored	Ya-Ate-Luo-Che

"WELCOME"

Word chart hanging
in a Seminole hut.

different, but they learned
to survive.

Today the Seminole have
adopted many modern
ways. But they have not
forgotten their Indian
heritage. They speak their
own language as well as
English.

There are state and federal Seminole reservations in southern Florida. Much of the land is swampy. However, at Brighton Reservation near Lake Okeechobee there is grazing land for a large herd of cattle. About four hundred Indians live on Brighton.

Big Cypress Reservation is farther south. Cattle are

The Brighton Reservation has modern homes (left) and a large herd of cattle (right).

also raised there. The men hunt and fish.

The council headquarters are at the Hollywood (Dania) Reservation. Visitors can tour a small model Seminole village.

Chickees in the model Seminole village near Tampa

Near Tampa, the Seminole have a large model village. Guides show how the Seminole lived years ago. These Indians hope to build a motel and restaurant to provide jobs and additional income.

To keep their Seminole culture alive, older people tell tribal legends to the young.

LIFE OFF THE RESERVATION

Some Indians prefer to live off the reservation. Many are very poor. Farming is difficult in the swampy area. They hunt and fish. Sometimes they

Air boats are used in the Everglades.

operate souvenir shops.
They also catch bullfrogs
and sell the frog legs to
restaurants in Miami.

Some families own air
boats that can skim over
the shallow water in the
Everglades. The men can

Seminole woman sews patchwork.

find better fishing grounds
from air boats than from
dugout canoes.

Women both on and off
the reservation make and
sell patchwork skirts,
dresses, and jackets in
shops.

SEMINOLE EDUCATION

For many years Seminole children had to attend the local school with non-Indian children.

Now there are schools on the reservations. The

Seminole children learn to read and write in their tribal language as well as English.

Seminole children learn to read and write in their own language as well as in English.

Many Seminole are Christians. They also keep many of their old ceremonies and dances. The important Green Corn Dance is held each year between May and July. It is the Seminole's harvest festival and a New Year's celebration.

Brilliant colors identify Seminole handicrafts.

Many Seminole dances are named for animals. They use few musical instruments, mainly drums and rattles made from turtle shells filled with small mud balls.

Seminole tribal headquarters in Hollywood, Florida

SEMINOLE GOVERNMENT

The Seminole have always had a democratic form of government.

Each village had a chief, or miko. Representatives from the different villages met in a council. Everyone

was allowed to speak at
the meetings.

All of the tribal members
vote for the principal chief
and vice-chief.

Mrs. Betty Mae Tiger
Jumper was the first
woman elected head of
the tribal council.

The federal government
helps the Indians through
the Bureau of Indian
Affairs. There is a great

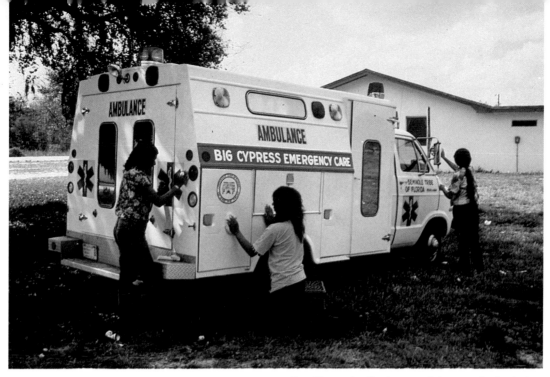

Continued efforts must be made to bring
better health services to the Seminole.

need to provide education
and job training. Health
services must be improved.

In 1968 the Seminole
joined the United
Southeastern Tribes of
North America to improve

Family ties are strong. When a Seminole
family makes a chickee (above) everyone works.

Supported by their rich tribal tradition, the Seminole can face the future with confidence.

life on Indian reservations. Led by Betty Mae Tiger Jumper, the Seminole plan to go more than "halfway to meet modern society."

45

WORDS YOU SHOULD KNOW

brave(BRAYV) — a warrior of an Indian tribe

chickee(CHIK • ee) — a hut with a raised platform, open sides, and thatched roof

community(kuh • MYOO • nih • tee) — a group of people living in the same area who have the same interests and life-style

council(KAUN • sill) — a group of leaders who represent those who elected or named them

descendants(di • SEN • dents) — people who are related to the same ancestor

desperate(DES • priht) — without hope; in great need of help

festival(FESS • tih • vul) — a celebration that features special events, games, entertainment, food, etc.

hammock(HAM • uk) — a piece of canvas or netting, fastened at the end so it swings, used for sleeping

heritage(HAIR • ih • tij) — a culture or way of life passed down by parents and other ancestors

patriot(PAY • tree • ut) — a person who loves and supports his country and countrymen

plantation(plan • TAY • shun) — a large farming estate worked by people who live on it

reservation(rez • er • VAY • shun) — a plot of land set aside by a government for use by Indians

runaway(RUN • uh • way) — a person or thing that runs away to escape from someone or something

settlers(SET • lerz) — people who have recently moved to an area to live

shallow(SHALL • oh) — not deep

slave(SLAYV) — a person who is owned by someone in the same way a thing is owned

surveyor(sir • VAY • er) — a person who surveys, or takes measurements of, certain areas or portions of land

tenant farmer (TEN • ent) — a farmer who works land owned by someone else; he pays rent either in cash or a portion of the crop he grows

treaty (TREET • ee) — an agreement made to promote peace

tribe (TRYBE) — a group ot people of the same race and with the same customs who band together under one leader

troops (TROOPS) — a group of soldiers

truce (TROOSS) — an agreement to stop fighting for a certain length of time

undergrowth (UN • der • groth) — small plants, shrubs, and grasses that grow low, under trees, on the floor of a forest

INDEX

About the author

Emilie Utteg Lepthien earned a BS and MA Degree and a certificate in school administration from Northwestern University. She has worked as an upper grade science and social studies teacher supervisor and a principal of an elementary and upper grade center for twenty years. Ms. Lepthien also has written and narrated science and social studies scripts for the Radio Council of the Chicago Board of Education.

Ms. Lepthien was awarded the American Educator's Medal by Freedoms Foundation. She is a member of the Delta Kappa Gamma Society International, Chicago Principals Association, and life member of the NEA. She has been a co-author of primary social studies texts for Rand, McNally and Co. and an educational consultant for Encyclopaedia Britannica Films.